A Kid's Guide to Cleopatra

An Book Just for Kids

eKids Press

www.eKidsPress.com

An Imprint of Minute Help, Inc.

Table of Content

ABOUT EKIDS 4

INTRODUCTION 6

CHAPTER 1: WHAT WAS IT LIKE TO BE A KID
WHEN CLEOPATRA LIVED?......................................8

CHAPTER 2: WHAT WAS CLEOPATRA LIKE AS
A KID 12

NOT AN EGYPTIAN?..14

HER EARLIEST YEARS...16

CHAPTER 3: WHAT WERE POLITICS AND
GOVERNMENT LIKE IN CLEOPATRA'S DAY?.19

EGYPTIAN LAW..21

EGYPTIAN POLITICS 22

CLEOPATRA'S EARLY POLITICAL EXPERIENCES 24

CHAPTER 4: WHO WAS JULIUS CAESAR AND
WHY IS HE IMPORTANT TO CLEOPATRA?......25

THE IMPORTANCE OF CAESAR 29

CHAPTER 5: WHO WAS MARK ANTONY AND
WHY IS HE IMPORTANT TO CLEOPATRA?......32

WHO WAS MARK ANTONY?..................................34

The Importance of Antony..36

CHAPTER 6: WHAT WAS THE ROMAN CIVIL WAR?..40

CHAPTER 7: HOW DID CLEOPATRA INFLUENCE THE ROMAN CIVIL WAR? 43

The Power of Cleopatra and Egypt......................45

The Battle of Actium..46

CHAPTER 8: HOW DID CLEOPATRA DIE?.........49

CONCLUSION 51

About eKids

Adults! Turn away! This book is not for you!

eKids Books is proud to present a new series of books for all the readers who matter the most: Kids, of course!

Introduction

Imagine if we had a President who was 15 years old when he/she took office. Imagine that it was a young girl, too. Imagine if that President could speak more than ten languages and ended up being married to two of the most powerful leaders of <u>other</u> governments during her time in office. Imagine if our leader then entered into a war with the largest nation on the planet...and lost that war.

This is exactly what happened to Cleopatra, or actually to Cleopatra VII Philopator, the very last pharaoh to rule Ancient Egypt.

She was a fascinating person born into an amazing world, but one that was very difficult to understand. Her family was always battling for power, and usually battling within the family itself. Brothers would have sisters murdered if it meant they could take control, and the dynasty to which Cleopatra belonged began with the famous Alexander the Great, and came to end when she died in 30 BC.

Why is she still so famous? Is it her legendary death by a poisonous snake? Is it her marriages to Caesar and Antony? Is it her incredible intelligence? We will discover that there are <u>many</u> reasons that we still know her name and continue to study her short but incredible life.

An ancient tomb painting showing daily life in Egypt.

Chapter 1: What Was it Like to be a Kid When Cleopatra Lived?

When you think about the life of an ancient Egyptian, what do you see in your mind's eye? Do you see slaves toiling in the brutal desert in order to build pyramids? Do you see luxurious palaces with gold, turquoise and rubies? Maybe you think of the pyramids and the Sphinx of Giza?

It is very interesting to learn that none of these things are what Cleopatra would have seen as a young girl. She was born in the year 69 BC in the city of Alexandria, which is on the northern coast of Egypt. She was actually from a Greek family and part of the dynasty started by Alexander the Great almost 300 years earlier. This means that Cleopatra was part of the Ptolemaic Dynasty and that she lived in the period of history known as the Hellenistic period. As she lived her life, however, she could not know that all of those words would be used to describe her lifetime because they did not yet exist. What she knew was that she was a member of the royal family of Egypt and that her father, Ptolemy XII Auletes was the Pharaoh.

She learned many languages as a child, and actually spent seven days each week in lessons. This meant that her life was very different from that of other children in Egypt. For example, in ancient times if a couple had no children of their own they would always adopt orphans. They would raise their child to be the heart of the family and to be kind and honest. Kids would learn about the world, how to do all of the things necessary for every day life, and they would learn that a light heart would bring eternal happiness. This is why all kids learned about ma'at (justice and order) and that if you did a bad deed you would need to rebalance things by making it right.

While this sounds very serious, it is important to remember that the ancient Egyptians really loved to celebrate life, the seasons and their families. There were always celebrations with music, food, swimming, sailing and dancing. Sadly, this meant that Cleopatra and her siblings did not get to enjoy the same kind of happy lives that most ancient Egyptian children did.

So, what was the typical day like in the life of an ancient Egyptian child? If you were a boy you would follow your father or uncles to their workshop or wherever they practiced a trade. This meant you might learn about the building trade, you might learn about the courts and laws, you might learn how to be a scribe (someone who wrote on tablets), a priest, someone in the army, and so much more.

If you were a young girl, on the other hand, you would have to stay home with your mother, sisters and other female family members. There you would learn how to do all of the work needed to keep the home.

Interestingly enough, some kids went to school in order to study religion, writing, math, and reading - but this was only if parents had enough money to do so. Even some girls were taught to read and write and to learn a special trade! Did they have an education like Cleopatra's? Not at all!

Chapter 2: What was Cleopatra Like as a Kid

Some experts might tell you that poor Cleopatra was never really a kid in the way that other kids are. She may have had some chances to play with other girls in the royal household, but it is not likely that she had a lot of free time to enjoy. Remember too that when she was 14 she became a co-ruler of Egypt, sharing this responsibility with her father. Though she would have had little actual power at that time she would still be viewed in the same way that a boy was.

In other words, Ancient Egyptians did not pass over females in any way - they inherited wealth and power. This was very unusual during this time in history, but a look at Egyptian history shows that there were many female leaders and authority figures.

So, that means that from the age of one to fourteen were the years Cleopatra was learning how to rule instead of playing games and having fun. Remember that the usual thing for an Egyptian kid to do was to follow their father to work in order to learn his trade. This means that Cleopatra would watch her father in the courts and as he worked as the leader of all of Egypt.

To help with her future job, she was taught many of the languages that she would need to be able to speak with her people. This meant that she knew how to speak her family's language: Greek. She had to learn the languages of the other inhabitants of Egypt as well, meaning: Hebrew, Ethiopian, Arabian, Syrian, Parthian, and even the language of the Egyptians. Remember that she mastered Latin and knew how to read in all of the languages she spoke!

It is important to point out Cleopatra's great intelligence at even a very early age. For example, she was unusual in her family because she did spend time learning to speak and read Egyptian in her early years. All of her other family members had refused to do this, which is why documents were always written in Egyptian hieroglyphics and in Greek, too. She changed this tradition and tried to show that she was one of the true Pharaohs because she spoke the tongue of the Egyptians. It is said that she had a great love of learning, and that it was her speaking that was more enchanting to those she met than her physical beauty was.

Not an Egyptian?

Remember that Cleopatra would have thought of herself as a Greek and not truly Egyptian. Her family spoke Greek to one another, and most never lived anywhere other than the coastal city of Alexandria. This was a place unlike the rest of Egypt because it was influenced by the different cultures that existed along the Mediterranean coast.

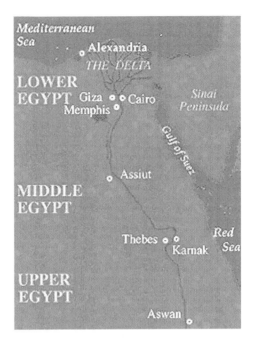

A map showing cities of
Ancient Egypt

For instance, the famous Library of Alexandria
was here. This was created by Cleopatra's
family, the Ptolemaic Dynasty. It was believed to
have most of the knowledge of the world in the
millions of scrolls, parchments and writings that
it contained. It was started by Ptolemy I Soter
sometime in the period dating around 200 BC,
but was accidentally destroyed by Julius Caesar
in 48 BC.

What this library shows, however, is that the people of Alexandria were dedicated scholars, while the remainder of Egypt was mostly concerned with purely Egyptian knowledge, culture and religion.

Because Cleopatra grew up in a city with this library it means that she was surrounded by all sorts of information from the outside world. This would really shape her education and help her in the years to come - particularly once she became a ruler of Egypt.

Her Earliest Years

Not a lot is known about Cleopatra's mother, who is thought to Cleopatra V Tryhpaena. This is not because she was unimportant or uninteresting but because the years the Cleopatra's father ruled Egypt were some of the most difficult imaginable. The court scribes were forever busy writing about the losses of land (such as Cyprus and Cyrenaica) and how the Pharaoh even lost his throne and had to flee to Rome. They also had to document their new leadership, and how the Pharaoh succeeded on his mission to Rome (to beg for support) and then returned three years later to reclaim his seat.

Imagine trying to grow up in such chaos...but that is what Cleopatra's childhood was like. It was during a trip to Rome (with Cleopatra at his side) that the Pharaoh's queen (Cleopatra's mother) died suddenly and mysteriously and Cleopatra never saw her again.

Not only that, but it was believed that her sister Berenice IV had been the person who ordered the death of her own mother. Why? Because she wanted to control Egypt! This was not unusual in those days, and even stranger things would happen shortly after this.

For instance, Ptolemy XII died in 51 BC, meaning that Cleopatra would become the ruler of Egypt at the age of 17 or 18. At the same time, she married her brother Ptolemy XIII (which was not an unusual thing to do in that time) because brothers were to share the throne according to their father's will.

So, by the age of 18 she had been a ruler for more than three years, travelled the world, learned a handful of languages, and studied for most of her life. Things would get even more interesting as time passed, and Cleopatra would soon lose her throne, fight to regain it, meet two of the most powerful men in the world, and become leader of an even greater empire.

To help to understand this, however, let's spend a bit of time learning about governments and politics during Cleopatra's time in Egypt...

Chapter 3: What Were Politics and Government Like in Cleopatra's Day?

If you learn about Ancient Egyptian politics and government, one of the first things that you discover is that they were very organized. Things were kept simple because everything depended upon one person - the Pharaoh. The entire Ancient Egyptian world was under the single Pharaoh who all citizens believed to be a living god.

So religion, culture, politics, law and the government all started at the top, with the Pharaoh. This means that in Ancient Egypt, politics and government were very different from things in other parts of the world. For example, the power of Egypt looked like this:

1. The Pharaoh

2. The Ministers and Government Officials of Egypt (Nobles and Army Officers as well as Court Officials)

3. Priests, Astrologers, Doctors and Priestesses

4. Scribes and Teachers

5. Architects and Engineers

6. Builders and Artisans

7. Soldiers and Army Leaders

8. Laborers, Fishermen, Farmers, and Tomb Builders (this is what MOST people did)

9. Slaves

Egyptians were very unique because they saw men and women (except slaves) as equals under the law. This meant that the government of Egypt would listen to the complaints or concerns of a peasant in the same way that they would listen to the concerns of a wealthy noble. The laws were very unique because everyone could own or sell property, sign or make contracts, get married and divorced, and receive an inheritance.

Consider that Cleopatra actually inherited the throne of all of Egypt from her father!

Was this so different from other governments and politics in the other countries of the time? Yes! For instance, if you were a woman in Ancient Rome or Greece you didn't enjoy any of the freedoms that the Ancient Egyptian women did. You could not rule or have a job in government, you did not often get an education, and you did not have the same rights of ownership, inheritance and more.

Egyptian Law

Ancient Egypt had an organized system of law, though very few documents or records survive showing the actual written laws. Instead, we already know that they believed in Ma'at or justice and order. This means that they had a basic system of right and wrong and what we would today call conflict resolution.

Basically, there were local councils that were called Kenbet, and they decided on all of the minor disputes and claims. If something was very serious, such as a murder or dispute over land, it would be sent to the Great Kenbet, which was ruled by a vizier or even by the Pharaoh. This means that the government was very directly involved in running the country at the local level.

This is important because the system could be a bit despotic. This means that a single ruler could make things unpleasant if he/she were greedy, selfish or unfair. This is why the equality of citizens was important - it kept them very loyal even if some cases did not result in a balanced solution.

Does this mean that things were always fair? By our modern understanding of the idea of fairness in the law, the Egyptian system was not so well balanced. After all, the courts could work as the judge and the prosecutor, and that means that someone could easily be accused and found guilty of a crime without actually having a fair trial.

Egyptian Politics

Though the Egyptian legal system was ruled by the Pharaoh, so too was the religious system. This means that all parts of Egyptian life were run by the king or Pharaoh, who was seen as the physical version of the many Egyptian gods.

Remember that the Egyptians did not exist for just a few hundred years, but a few thousand years. Their nation was invaded many times, but their form of government and politics was able to restore peace many times over. In fact, many believe that the blend of religion, politics and government is what allowed the country to remain so powerful for so many thousands of years.

By the time Cleopatra came to the throne, however, Egypt was very weak and at the end of what we call the Pharaonic Period. We know that Cleopatra was the very last of the pharaohs, and that greater forces outside of her country were trying to influence her government.

For example, her own father had to ask Rome to help him to take back his throne in the years before he died. Earlier pharaohs would not have had to ask for help. This means that the well organized Egyptian system had already failed by the time Cleopatra came to power.

She too would have to ask for help from outsiders over the years she reigned as the ruler of Egypt. In fact, the very reason she ended up fighting for her throne had to do with politics and governments outside of Egypt.

Cleopatra's Early Political Experiences

We have already learned that there was an order to the way that Egypt was governed and that the nobles and priests were supposed to follow the orders of their pharaoh. Unfortunately, many of these people became corrupt and wanted power and wealth for themselves. To get this they would often try to put other people on the throne through such things as murder or political trouble.

This is precisely what happened to Cleopatra in the earliest years after her father's death. He died in 51 BC and by 48 BC (three years later) she had to flee her home and head to Syria to remain safe. This is because some of the court's officials decided to work to get her younger brother on the throne and to eliminate the older Cleopatra altogether.

So, in the first years of her reign, poor Cleopatra lost her father, had to leave her homeland, and had to begin working to build an army that could help her to reclaim control. She literally went from a comfortable life in the palace where she ruled a large country to a tent in a desert where she scraped together enough loyal soldiers to begin to move against her own brother.

Chapter 4: Who Was Julius Caesar and Why is he Important to Cleopatra?

At the exact same time that Cleopatra was running from Alexandria and trying to find a way to return to her throne, Julius Caesar and Pompey were fighting over leadership of the entire Roman Empire.

They were involved in what is known as a civil war. This is a war that happens between two groups in the same country or republic. Usually it is a war in which the groups are fighting for control of the entire country or to change the way that the government operates.

It was actually a pretty common thing in Ancient Rome, too, and what happened during Cleopatra's rule was very interesting. Pompey had actually been defeated by Caesar and had decided to run to Egypt and Ptolemy XIII for help. The defeated leader had been chosen by the Roman Senate as a guardian of Egypt, and this made him believe that he would be saved once he landed in Alexandria.

Pompey was wrong and he had barely stepped from the waters of the Mediterranean to the beach of Alexandria when he was murdered by order of the pharaoh. This was something that the Romans would not tolerate, even if they were at war with one another.

Julius Caesar left for Alexandria only a few days after the murder and ordered both Cleopatra and her brother to meet with him. This would have been very difficult for Cleopatra because it would mean finding a way to re-enter the country and to risk being captured by her brother's forces.

To avoid what would have been a certain death, she had one of her most loyal friends help her sneak into Alexandria and the royal palace, where Julius Caesar was staying. Legends and histories tell us that she was rolled up in an old carpet and carried on her friend Apollodorus's shoulder directly into Caesar's chambers.

This guaranteed that she would reach the Emperor unharmed and that she would have a chance to explain her side of the story. Many believe that Caesar immediately fell in love with the beautiful queen, but many also think it was her sharp mind and honesty that won him over, too. Either way, Caesar chose Cleopatra's side of the argument and put her back in control with another brother serving as a co-ruler.

Of course, things were not as easy as that. Cleopatra's brother did meet with Caesar and the Queen, and understood immediately that Caesar would choose Cleopatra as the ruler. He tried to flee the meeting to prevent this and was taken prisoner by the Roman forces. This led to a siege of the royal palace in the city, and eventually Caesar released Ptolemy. This did not bring the siege to an end for another six months, but the Romans prevailed and Cleopatra was returned to power, and again married another younger brother.

Ptolemy XIII had died by accidental drowning when he fled the city after Caesar gave Cleopatra control of Egypt, and now it was another brother, Ptolemy XIV, who sat alongside his older sister on the throne. The two would rule peacefully together, and would even pay a visit to Caesar in Rome in 44 BC.

We know now that Cleopatra wanted to be in Rome because she and Caesar had a son together - Caesarion. He was born in 46 BC and was around two when he was in Rome with his parents. By the time they arrived in the city Caesar had been named dictator of the Roman Empire for his lifetime. This made a lot of people dangerously jealous of him. Sadly, Cleopatra and her son (along with her brother) were all in the city when Caesar was murdered by members of the Senate in March of 44 BC. This put the Egyptian rulers at risk and they fled the city.

The Importance of Caesar

Julius Caesar was a famous leader of Rome who fell in love with Cleopatra and who put her back in control of Egypt. Without his friendship and support she would have surely never been able to return to the throne.

Although Cleopatra's first husband, her brother Ptolemy XIII, had guaranteed the end of his own reign in Egypt by murdering the Roman leader Pompey and sending his head to Caesar as evidence, it is unknown if Caesar would have chosen Cleopatra over her brother. It was her courage and determination to sneak into the palace and negotiate for her throne that won him over.

When they left Egypt to travel to Rome, Caesar had placed Roman forces all over Egypt to ensure that Cleopatra was indeed going to remain the ruling pharaoh. This plan worked, and she was able to stay in control of Egypt in the two years following the murder of Caesar.

Things back in Rome were not so calm because major forces were battling for control over the Empire. Many thought that Caesar had named a leading politician and general, Mark Antony, as his heir. He had not done this, and his will had actually named one of his relatives, Octavian, as the leader. At the time of his murder Octavian formed an alliance with Mark Antony and another man named Lepidus. This was known as the Second Triumvirate that was meant to rule the Empire in an organized manner. It only lasted a few years and by 33 BC the union was dissolved. By that time, however, Mark Antony had met and also fallen in love with Cleopatra. This was something that would have a large impact on Egypt and the system of pharaohs.

Why? Because Cleopatra was so close to Antony, and because Rome was in the midst of a civil war, it linked everything together in unusual ways. For example, could Cleopatra have saved Egypt if she had not been in love with Antony? Would Rome have been kinder to Egypt if the pharaoh was not linked directly to one of the rebellious leaders of the empire?

To answer those questions we have to learn about Mark Antony and why he was so important to Cleopatra.

Chapter 5: Who Was Mark Antony and Why is He Important to Cleopatra?

When people talk about the greatest love stories in history they often say Antony and Cleopatra. You don't usually hear Cleopatra and Caesar even though she had a son with this Emperor and knew him for most of her adult life.

So, what makes the love story of Antony and Cleopatra so famous? Well, you should know that it does NOT have a happy ending. They both killed themselves in 30 BC after the famous Battle of Actium. They also had to endure many years of civil war and long times spent apart.

The reason that so many people consider their story to be an epic romance is simple: they loved each other so much that they almost forgot that they were rulers of enormous empires or nations. Though they fought battles and attempted to win control of their governments, they would also end up losing everything because of their devotion to one another.

Who Was Mark Antony?

Before the murder of Julius Caesar in 44 BC, the Roman Empire was run by its Dictator for Life (Caesar) and the Senate. This means that there were a lot of politicians, ideas, and jealousies in the city of Rome. One group of senators was so jealous of Caesar that they murdered him and worked to divide the Roman Empire.

They only partially succeeded because Caesar's will did name an heir - a cousin by the name of Octavian, but this man chose to work with Mark Antony and Lepidus to create the Second Triumvirate that would rule three equal parts of the Empire. Things were never simple for this group, and it would take only a few years before a power struggle between Octavian and Antony occurred.

It wasn't that helpful that Antony was married to Octavian's sister, but was living with Cleopatra in Egypt most of the time. The Roman world felt that this was a scandal and did not view Antony as a good person at all.

Consider too that Cleopatra and Antony also had three children together during this time. This was also viewed as a very bad thing, but we have to consider how both of them looked at marriage.

For example, Cleopatra had been forced to marry her brothers. This was never a romantic marriage and she never lived a normal life with them. There were never any children and the marriages were only for a political reason - to ensure the power of the throne. The same can be said about Antony who married Octavian's sister as a way of making peace and keeping his power in the Triumvirate. This too was not a romantic marriage.

So, it may have been wrong that Cleopatra and Antony were living together and raising a family, but we have to always remember the time that they lived in and the ways that their lives had been pushed and pulled by politics.

The Importance of Antony

Why was Mark Antony important to Cleopatra? We know that Caesar was killed in 44 BC and that Cleopatra fled back to Egypt that same year. We know that she ruled Egypt peacefully for the next two years, and that in 41 BC she was summoned by Antony to a place known as Tarsus in order to discuss forming some sort of political union. It was then that they actually fell in love.

This means that almost from the very start both Cleopatra and Antony were not only acting for political reasons but trying to find ways to be together. Unfortunately, a lot of issues came between them and forced them to think first of their roles as leaders and then as people who cared for one another.

So, Antony would marry Octavian's sister to keep the peace, and Cleopatra would give money to Roman causes and wars, even if that meant that Antony might face grave dangers and total failure.

While Antony was fighting wars with the Parthians and seeking to defend Roman territory, he was losing support and control in Rome. In fact, while he was on the retreat from the Parthians in Armenia, the Triumvirate was being dissolved by Octavian. It was then that Antony's behaviors towards Cleopatra began to have an influence on world history.

For example, Octavian was considered to be in control of the Roman empire, and he began to talk about Antony in many bad ways. He then summoned (demanded) that Antony return to Rome and discuss the new government that was being formed. Not only did Antony refuse, but he remained in Egypt with Cleopatra for many months. He had made his way there from Armenia (to Alexandria) and had been promised the money he needed to continue battling the Parthians from there.

He felt so strongly that he formally announced the end of the Triumvirate and named his children as the leaders of the territory he had conquered. He also pointed out that Caesarian was the son of Caesar, and was the true leader of the Roman Empire - not Octavian.

Most experts believe that if Antony had only given the lands to his children he would have avoided a permanent break with Rome, but challenging Octavian's rule by naming Caesar's son as the true Emperor was too much. This was even more upsetting to the Romans because Caesarian's mother was the world's richest and most powerful woman. This meant she might put together an army and re-take the Roman holdings for her son, and that many would support her as she did it.

This means that Antony's importance in the story of Cleopatra is that he fell in love with her, had children with her, and decided that he would separate himself from Rome in order to attempt to re-shape the world with her by his side. This was something that history had never witnessed, and it led to a major clash of powers known as the Final War of the Roman Republic.

A sculpture of Octavian

Chapter 6: What was the Roman Civil War?

Antony's war, the Roman Civil War or the Final War of the Roman Republic are all the same thing. Basically it was a war between Cleopatra and Octavian, but was really the result of one act: the famous Donations of Alexandria.

This was seen as a major betrayal by Mark Antony when he ceded or gave a huge amount of Roman territory to Cleopatra (by naming her children the official leaders of major pieces of land). For example, Cyprus was handed over to Cleopatra and Caesarian; Libya and Cyrenaica were given to their daughter; and Syria and Phoenicia to another son.

These things were not severe enough to make all of the Roman Senate feel that a declaration of war against Egypt was necessary. Yes, it was shocking that Antony simply handed over Roman territory and also that it went to his own children, but it was even more shocking when he decided to actually marry Cleopatra.

That is the one step that many historians feel drove the two countries to war. Though a lot of gossip had occurred about Antony and Cleopatra, the fact that he had not yet divorced Octavian's sister and was making plans to marry Cleopatra was just too much. When it was also discovered that he was going to try to create another Senate in the city of Alexandria, most people felt he was going to ruin the Roman Empire. Octavian used this moment to ensure that Antony would be viewed as a traitor and read his will to the Senate. In it, Antony said that Caesarian was the legal Roman Emperor, not Octavian. This meant that some could say that Antony was acting as a traitor. Soon, the Senate declared war against Cleopatra simply because she was the leader of another nation and because they knew Antony would help her fight any battles.

Octavian's plan worked because the moment that Egypt learned of the declaration of war against Cleopatra, Mark Antony declared his loyalty to Egypt and not to his homeland of Rome. This led the Senate to remove all of Antony's legal powers and to label him officially as a traitor. He was no longer to be called a Roman, and no longer to be a leader of any Roman forces.

The Battle of Actium

Chapter 7: How Did Cleopatra Influence the Roman Civil War?

It is interesting to note that Cleopatra actually influenced two different Roman Civil Wars. The first was the war between the men who had murdered Caesar, and the men who would quickly take control of Rome - Antony, Octavian and Lepidus. The murderers were quickly conquered and fled east of the empire.

They had initially appealed to Cleopatra for support, but she obviously refused to offer anything at all. When one of them made it clear that they would invade Egypt in an attempt to punish the pharaoh for her refusal, Cleopatra set sail to join with Antony and the others. A storm ruined many of her ships and forced her enemies to head to the Adriatic Sea.

Though this does not seem like much of an influence at all, it is clear that Cleopatra's obvious support for the Caesarians would help her to remain in their favor even after the death of Caesar. This also proved to Antony that Cleopatra was loyal to Rome and could be trusted.

In the second civil war, or the Final War of the Roman Republic, she had much stronger influence over the outcome. For one thing, she was with Antony when he handed over huge pieces of Roman territory to his children. This made many Romans see her as a trouble maker and an enemy to their empire. She also accepted the role of leader in many of the lands that Antony was taking with him as he left the Triumvirate. This made her even more of an enemy to Rome.

Remember that she also had a son with Julius Caesar, and that he was the only legal heir to his father's throne. This threatened the leadership in place in Rome, and made all of Octavian's actions questionable. It is also important to remember that she was still a very wealthy and powerful person and that she could easily build armies and begin to conquer enormous areas of the empire if that is what she had in mind.

All of these thoughts drove Octavian to constantly appeal to the Senate to view her as a threat and to declare war against her. Not everyone felt that this was the right thing to do, but when she married Mark Antony it made most Romans believe that the loyalty of both Antony and Cleopatra had shifted permanently to Egypt and away from Rome altogether.

They could accept a pharaoh with powerful children and a great deal of wealth, but one that was deeply loyal to Egypt and not Rome was a clear threat. Because it was said that she had turned Antony against Rome, it was even easier for the Senate to get a declaration of war against the Queen of Egypt.

The Power of Cleopatra and Egypt

Once the declaration was made and Cleopatra and Antony heard the news, the power of her wealth became clear. Antony had some loyal soldiers, but this was no match to the fighting power of Egypt.

Cleopatra had her nation's military forces behind her, and that meant naval vessels and even hired soldiers if required. Unfortunately, Rome was able to pull more than two hundred thousand soldiers into the fight, and this offset things quite a bit.

For example, the war was fought on land and sea. Though the numbers were equal, the Egyptian forces under Antony were not as experienced at naval combat as the Romans. The Egyptians had large vessels, but these could not compete with small and fast ships sailed by the experienced Roman army. This meant that the naval battles would not be easily won by Antony and his forces.

So, though the number of soldiers and the amount of money available for the war was even on both sides, the lack of experience in sea battles would eventually bring Antony to disaster.

The Battle of Actium

In 31 BC, Mark Antony would face the Romans in a sea battle off of the coast of Actium. Cleopatra too was present for this battle and had brought many ships of her own. It is important to know that Octavian had tried to negotiate with Antony before this battle, but Antony and Cleopatra had refused. This was unfortunate because it meant that this sea battle would end up being an all or nothing event.

There were months of preparations before the actual day of the battle, but on the morning of September 2 they finally began to attack one another. Antony had more than 500 vessels, and Octavian had around 250 special warships. The Romans had the best position and their ships were manned properly. This means that there were enough soldiers on each ship to make them very effective. For Antony, things were different and his many large vessels did not have enough men on board to make them good for a fight.

Even before the fight started some of Antony's men recognized that they might easily lose the day, and defected to the Roman army. One of them actually gave Antony's battle plans to the enemy!

The battle raged most of the morning, and by afternoon it was clear that Antony was going to lose. Many historians debate what happened next, but most know that Cleopatra signaled her ships to retreat and to head back to the open sea. Antony was not told why the Egyptians were disappearing but believed it was because they had lost the battle. Soon he had also retreated and escaped through the enemy lines.

This did not end the war, and Octavian quickly made his way to Alexandria in order to capture Antony and Cleopatra and take control of Egypt. So many of Antony's soldiers left before the battle that Antony is said to have given up hope and stabbed himself. There are different tales, but most agree that he was with Cleopatra when he died.

She was allowed to give him a proper funeral (even though she was now a prisoner of Octavian). Because she knew that Octavian would take Egypt and bring her to Rome as a prize of war, she too decided to end her own life.

Chapter 8: How Did Cleopatra Die?

There are many debates about the actual way that Cleopatra died. Since we don't even know where she was buried, no tomb has ever been found, and we cannot say exactly what happened.

What we do know is that there are two different tales that come from people who were alive at the time she died. One of the tales is that she used a poisonous snake (some stories say a cobra and others say an asp) hidden in a basket of figs to kill herself. The story is that a loyal servant prepared the basket and brought it to the Queen. She then stuck her hand into the basket to allow the snake to bite her, and then she died shortly afterward. The second tale says that she used a combination of very powerful poisons to kill herself.

A historian named Strabos was also in Alexandria when Cleopatra died and he adds yet another version of the story. He says that many spoke of poisonous creams that the Queen used to end her own life.

What really happened? We may never know the truth about her death because of the passage of time, the absence of documents that give formal details, and the fact that poets, song writers, and storytellers all began to create stories about her almost immediately after she died.

We have to also remember that many of the histories written about her were actually written by her enemies. This makes it hard to know the truth from mean gossip or tall tales.

Her conqueror, Octavian, did help to spread the story about the death by snake because he had a statue of Cleopatra in his victory parade. That statue was shown to have a poisonous asp biting the Queen, which is why so many began to immediately believe that she did indeed die after being bitten by a snake.

What we do know is the Cleopatra lived, changed the world in many ways, and then took her own life. Until we find her final resting place we will never know exactly what happened or how she really died. For now, we can choose the story we like best - we might believe the stories as written by Plutarch, Shakespeare, hundreds of other poets or playwrights and more.

Upon her death her son Caesarion was immediately named as the new pharaoh, but he was captured by Octavian as soon as Alexandria fell too. No one knows what happened to the young man, but we do know that Antony's wife did take responsibility of all three of the children born to Cleopatra and Antony. They were raised as Romans and one of the daughters was even married to a King of Numidia!

Egypt became a province of Rome upon her death and was not independent again until the twentieth century.

Conclusion

Something interesting to know about the Egyptians and their view of death is that if you say the name of the dead it is as if they were brought to life again. Just think of how many millions of times Cleopatra is remembered...if the Egyptians were right, Cleopatra will live forever!

The last pharaoh of Egypt was the great queen
Cleopatra. She is a huge figure in history and in
culture. There are few people who do not know
her name and at least a bit of her story. While
there are arguments about whether or not she
was a real beauty, how many languages she
spoke, and if she truly loved Caesar or Antony,
we can say that she has influenced many
different things in the modern world.

From cosmetics, clothing and hairstyles
Cleopatra has created many different ideas and
views about what it means to be beautiful. From
politics, education and government she has also
shown the world what an intelligent woman can
do. Because of that, we don't need to know how
she died, but only appreciate that she lived.

Cover Image © redav - Fotolia.com

Made in United States
Orlando, FL
21 November 2021

10567889R00033